Mom, Dad, I'm Living With A White Girl

by Marty Chan

Playwrights Canada Press
Toronto•Canada

Mom, Dad, I'm Living With A White Girl © Copyright 1995 Marty Chan

Playwrights Canada Press
215 Spadina Ave. Suite 230
Toronto, Ontario CANADA M5T 2C7
(416) 703-0013 fax (416) 408-3402
info@puc.ca http://www.puc.ca

Playwrights Canada Press acknowledges the support of
The Canada Council for the Arts for our publishing programme and
the Ontario Arts Council.

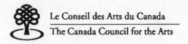

Le Conseil des Arts du Canada
The Canada Council for the Arts

ONTARIO ARTS COUNCIL
CONSEIL DES ARTS DE L'ONTARIO

Cover photo of Caroline Livingstone and Jared Matsunaga-Turnbull by
Ian Jackson.
Production Manager: Jodi Armstrong

Canadian Cataloguing in Publication Data

Chan, Marty,
 Mom, dad, I'm living with a white girl

A play.
ISBN 0-88754-614-5

I. Title

PS8553.H225M65 2001   C812'.6   C2001-930000-X
PR9199.3.C42M65 2001

First edition: April 2001
Second Printing: January 2005
Printed and bound by Hignell Printing at Winnipeg, Manitoba, Canada.

Dedication:

To Michelle, who stayed.

PLAYWRIGHT'S ACKNOWLEDGEMENTS

If you're reading this, you've either worked on the show and are looking for your name; or you're interested in my acknowledgements. I'm sorry I didn't mention your name.

My grateful thanks to: Alberta Foundation for the Arts; Ontario Arts Council; Laidlaw Foundation; Department of Canadian Heritage; Air Canada; Toronto Arts Council; The Canada Council for the Arts; Cahoots Theatre; Sally Han; Donna Spencer; Ben Henderson; and Colin Page.

My sincere apologies to: Mom, Dad and the white girl.

The Toronto premiere of *Mom, Dad, I'm Living with a White Girl* was produced by Cahoots Theatre in association with Theatre Passe Muraille on March 16, 1995. The original cast and crew were:

Mark Gee	Arthur Eng
Li Fen Gee	Brenda Kamino
Kim Gee	Paul Lee
Sally Davis	Linda Prystawska
Director	Sally Han
Set Design	Bill Rassmussen
Lighting Design	Aisling Sampson
Sound Design	Victor Oland
Stage Manager	Maria Costa

The Vancouver premiere of *Mom, Dad, I'm Living with a White Girl* was produced by Firehall Arts Centre on Feburary 1, 1996. The cast and crew were:

Mark Gee	Daniel Chen
Li Fen Gee	Donna Yamamoto
Kim Gee	John James Hong
Sally Davis	Kirsten Robek
Director	Donna Spencer
Set and Lighting	Stephen Allen
Sound Design	Stephen Bulat
Stage Manager	Angela Kirk

Running with Scissors Theatre toured western Canada with *Mom, Dad, I'm Living with a White Girl* in 2000 - 2001 with the following cast and crew:

Mark Gee	Jared Matsunaga-Turnbull
Li Fen Gee	Laara Ong
Kim Gee	Patrick Gallagher
Sally Davis	Caroline Livingstone
Drummer	Peter Moller/Chris Craddock
Director	Ben Henderson
Production Design	Robert Shannon
Sound Design	Peter Moller
Stage Manager	Shauna Murphy

CHARACTERS

KIM GEE   45
LI FEN GEE   40
MARK GEE   20
SALLY DAVIS   22
DRUMMER

ACT ONE

The lines between fact and fiction blur. Nightmares intrude upon reality until one cannot be distinguished from the other. Fear dominates reason. This is the twisted world of MARK.

Reflecting his nightmares, the set looks like an evil lair of the Yellow Claw, an Oriental warlord bent on world domination, but it can also function as various homes and an acupuncture clinic. A torture rack doubles as kitchen table and acupuncture table. There are four imperious chairs around the table, facing each other, two against two.

On the outskirts of the set, a DRUMMER provides all the sound and music. His main instrument is a Chinese gong. He rings it, summoning KIM.

KIM comes out with a balloon in one hand and a long needle in the other. The balloon is painted with the continents of the world. North America faces the audience.

Behind KIM, LI FEN lurks in the shadows, with a cigarette in a long cigarette holder.

KIM	The key is the entry point. Find the right one and we can reach the nerve centre. Strike where they are most vulnerable. Ah. The heart of decadence. Vancouver. Yellow Claw, we will infiltrate their society as a moth chews through silk.
LI FEN	Not infiltrate. The east shall overcome the west.
KIM	Yellow Claw, can't we insinuate ourselves into their world with Dim Sum buffets and Chinese take out?
LI FEN	No, Kim. Two worlds cannot coincide. We must conquer or submit.
KIM	Ah... you are wise as you are evil, mistress.

LI FEN	Nothing can stop me from worldwide domination.
KIM	Nothing.

LI FEN and KIM laugh. LI FEN flicks her cigarette. He inserts the needle into the globe.

The globe turns yellow. Smoke billows out – white at first, then turning yellow. LI FEN exits, laughing. KIM follows.

MARK sneaks on stage. He wears a trenchcoat.

SALLY enters in a trenchcoat. She is enveloped by the fog. A figure shrouded in mystery and intrigue.

SALLY	The canary flies the coop at midnight.
MARK	The panda devours her cubs.
SALLY	The cocoon suffocates the butterfly.
MARK	The young tree has deep roots.
SALLY	Agent Banana?
MARK	Snow Princess?
SALLY	So you wish to defect from the ranks of the Yellow Claw?
MARK	Yes, I seek independence. The right to speak my mind. And the apathy to say nothing.
SALLY	Ah, you wish to be Canadian. Well, there is a price you must pay for this.
MARK	Anything.
SALLY	As a servant of the Yellow Claw, you surely must know something of her weaknesses.
MARK	She is an inscrutable villain.

SALLY   Agent Banana, you must know of some way to destroy her. For the sake of the western world.

MARK   There might be a way to hurt her, Snow Princess.

SALLY   Yes?

DRUMMER   (*echoing*) Yes, yes, yes.

SALLY   How?

DRUMMER   (*echoing*) How, how, how.

MARK kisses SALLY full on the lips.

Crash of gong.

Agent Banana and Snow Princess become MARK and SALLY. She pulls away.

SALLY   Mark, people can see...

MARK   So? Who cares, Sally?

SALLY   The lady on the park bench. What's got into you tonight?

MARK   I'm high on you.

SALLY   You bullshitter. Keep talking.

MARK   I can't get enough of you, Sally. You're like oxygen.

SALLY   Then breathe me in. Oh God, did that sound as lame to you as it did to me?

MARK   Yeah. Wanna head to the beach?

SALLY   How about a movie instead? There's an Ang Lee running at the Ridge.

MARK   I hate subtitles.

SALLY	Mark, he's a Hollywood director now.
MARK	Let's go. Just for an hour. We can rent a John Woo flick after.
SALLY	Not in a million years. Forget the beach, Mark. It's too cold.
MARK	(*Pause.*) Sally, where do you see us going?
SALLY	I was hoping the movies. (*beat*) I thought we were having a good time.
MARK	Am I a boyfriend or a movie buddy?
SALLY	There's nothing wrong with just letting things happen.
MARK	It's been a year. I figured there'd be something more by now.
SALLY	Like what?
MARK	Something.
SALLY	Oh great. Let me know when you figure it out, okay?
MARK	Forget it.
SALLY	What's been bugging you lately? Is it the fact that I'm always paying for everything?
MARK	Let's just go to your stupid movie.
SALLY	I'm the one who's working. You're not going to pull some kind of macho head trip on me, are you?
MARK	Just drop it, okay?
SALLY	What is your big problem?
MARK	I love you.

SALLY	Oh.
MARK	Thanks for sharing.
SALLY	You don't blurt out something like that in the middle of a fight.
MARK	Believe me, that's not how I planned it.
SALLY	I didn't think you felt this way.
MARK	Well, now you know.
SALLY	You're serious?
MARK	Sally, I've been with you longer than anyone else. How can you think I'm not?
SALLY	Two months ago. Remember? Dinner with my dad?
MARK	Yeah...?
SALLY	I cared enough to subject you to my family.
MARK	Uh huh.
SALLY	Don't you get it? I showed you mine, but you never showed me yours. Why not?

Crash of gong.

MARK	Snow Princess, we shouldn't have succumbed to our primal desires.
SALLY	But Agent Banana, sweet is the fruit that is forbidden.
MARK	Oh... Snow Princess, you are my queen.
SALLY	My little banana.
MARK	Um, maybe we should drop our code names.

SALLY	Call me Sally.
MARK	Mark.
SALLY	Ah, a strong name. Like Mark Antony. Successor to Caesar. Ruler of Rome. Consort of Cleopatra.
MARK	Sally. Sally? Sally...
SALLY	Your concise passion takes my breath away.

She kisses him. KIM enters.

KIM	Infidel! Betrayer!
SALLY	Do you mind?
MARK	Careful! It's the Yellow Claw's henchman. Kim Gee.
KIM	My mistress sends her greetings. Hiya!

KIM holds up a shuriken and throws it with deadly force. SALLY grabs her forehead. A shuriken is imbedded there. She turns to MARK.

SALLY	Smells like highly concentrated opium. It will knock out an adult in three sec– unh!

She passes out and flops to the ground.

MARK	Snow Princess? Sally? Wake up.
KIM	The price for consorting with the white devil is certain and slow death.
MARK	I would never betray the Yellow Claw.
KIM	Liar. What have you told the infidel?
MARK	Nothing.
KIM	You will talk.

MARK   Never.

KIM   Then you will break like so many Taiwanese toys.
            Hiya!

> KIM *hurls the shuriken. MARK ducks. A*
> *ricochet sound as the shuriken bounces off the*
> *DRUMMER's gong. The DRUMMER is caught*
> *off guard.*

DRUMMER Hey! Aim! Fucker!

KIM   So sorry. Hiya!

> KIM *holds up a shuriken and throws it. MARK*
> *clutches his forehead – the shuriken is there. He falls*
> *beside SALLY.*

> *Crash of gong as KIM backs out.*

> MARK *and* SALLY *sit up.*

SALLY   Mark, everyone has trouble with their parents.

MARK   Not like mine.

SALLY   Do you think my mother and I are soul mates?
            Hallmark doesn't have enough cards to cover the
            crap she pulls.

MARK   Trust me, Sally. The less I see of them, the longer
            they'll live.

SALLY   Okay, fine. Whatever. I'm just telling you why
            I didn't think you were serious.

MARK   I want us to go on, Sally.

SALLY   Then introduce me to them. I promise I won't
            embarrass you.

MARK   It's not you I'm worried about.

SALLY	Come on, let me impress them. I'll wow them with my Cantonese.
MARK	You'll call my mom a prostitute by mistake.
SALLY	My Chinese is good, swo ji [*silly boy*].
MARK	I told you.
SALLY	(*laughs*) Mark... just give me a chance.
MARK	Anything else, Sally.
SALLY	If you're serious about us, this is it.

Lights crossfade to the table. MARK and SALLY watch as LI FEN enters and sets the table. She does everything with ritual, even when she places the chairs around the table.

A tinkle. MARK gets up with SALLY. LI FEN sees MARK.

MARK	Hey Mom. Hope we're not late.
LI FEN	(*sees SALLY*) Aiya. This the friend you talk about?
SALLY	Hi, Mrs. Gee.
MARK	Mom, this is Sally. Sally, my mom.
SALLY	It's a pleasure to meet you, Mrs. Gee.
LI FEN	(*to MARK*) Aiya, nay mo waa nay ge pungyow hi gwai leur. [*You didn't tell me your friend is a girl.*]
MARK	Where's dad?
LI FEN	Downstairs. In clinic.
SALLY	I've been dying to meet you, Mrs. Gee.
LI FEN	Look like we have much to talk about.

MARK	Sally should meet dad first.
LI FEN	You go get him.
SALLY	Yeah, it'll give your mom and me a chance to chat. I'd love to learn more about your culture, Mrs. Gee.
LI FEN	Yes. I want to know more about you too.
MARK	Dad!!!! Dinner's on!!!
LI FEN	Mark. Go down and get him.
MARK	Dad!!!!

KIM enters.

KIM	Aiya, what is so important– Oh...
MARK	Dad, this is Sally.
KIM	Hello. Wife, I'm hungry. Hurry up.

LI FEN exits.

SALLY	It's great to meet you, Mr. Gee.
MARK	We should have supper. I can't stay long.

MARK hangs up SALLY and his trenchcoats.

KIM	What else is new?
LI FEN	Make your dad happy. Stay little longer.
SALLY	Mark, I'd like to get to know your parents better.
LI FEN	That be nice.

LI FEN enters with three dishes of Chinese food on a tray. She sets them on the table.

KIM	Mark, get me some tea.

MARK	What's wrong with your legs?
LI FEN	Aiya, I get it.
SALLY	Need a hand, Mrs. Gee?
MARK	She knows her way around the kitchen, Sally.
SALLY	I want to help.
LI FEN	You guest. Food ready. You start eating.
SALLY	Let me peek over your shoulder then. I'd love to see how you make authentic Chinese tea.
LI FEN	You pour hot water on tea leaves.

LI FEN exits.

KIM	Sit. Eat.
MARK	So. How are you?
KIM	Busy. Everyone looking for acupuncture now.
SALLY	If you're swamped, you should get someone to help. You know, I've always had an interest in acupuncture. Maybe I could free up a weekend or two and learn about your job, Mr. Gee.
KIM	Thank you, but better to keep it in family.
MARK	I'm a mechanic, Dad.
KIM	No, you are unemployed.

Silence. Awkward silence. LI FEN enters with a tea pot.

LI FEN	Tea is ready. Mark, why you not eat?
MARK	We were waiting for you.
LI FEN	Food getting cold. Eat. (*to SALLY*) You need fork?

SALLY	I'm fine with chopsticks, Mrs. Gee. This is quite the feast. Do you always feed Mark so well?
KIM	He always get the best. Whether he deserves it or not.
LI FEN	No more talk. Eat.

Everyone eats. SALLY proves to be dexterous with the chopsticks.

SALLY	Mmmm, it's delicious. This l'aw bok goh. Ho may doe.
LI FEN	What?
SALLY	Ho may doe. It's very good.
MARK	Sally knows Cantonese.
LI FEN	Mark teach you?
SALLY	No, I'm taking a few courses. Chinese history. Politics. And language.
KIM	Very good. Smart girl.
LI FEN	Yes... you speak good.
SALLY	D'aw je.
LI FEN	What she call me?
MARK	She said thank you.
LI FEN	Welcome.
SALLY	Mmmm, this dish is wonderful.
LI FEN	Shrimp too dry.
SALLY	No, no. They're perfectly moist.
LI FEN	You too kind. Have some more rice.

SALLY	No thank you, Mrs. Gee.
LI FEN	No?
MARK	She's a light eater, Mom.
SALLY	What did I do wrong?

Crash of gong.

LI FEN	I offer you a share of my humble dinner, and you spurn my invitation of hospitality. How rude.
MARK	She's not rude. She's Canadian.
KIM	Eat the rice.
LI FEN	I am only being a good host.
SALLY	You call drugging and dragging us to your den of deception hospitable?
LI FEN	I only wanted the boy, but someone failed to obey me.
KIM	Uh... eat the rice.
SALLY	Never.
LI FEN	Come now, what possible evil could I be up to?

SALLY holds up a grain and sniffs it.

SALLY	Aha! Truth serum. Slipped a few almonds in so we wouldn't detect the scent, eh? Too bad you used West Indian instead of Hawaiian.
KIM	Yellow Claw, they refuse to eat from the rice bowl of a thousand truths.
LI FEN	Curses.
MARK	Yellow Claw, you are devious.

Crash of gong.

left to right:

Laara Ong,
Jared
Matsunaga-
Turnbull,
Caroline
Livingstone,
Patrick
Gallagher.

photo by Ian
Jackson

KIM	Eat some more rice, Sally.
LI FEN	If she full, she full.

LI FEN clears the table lightning fast.

SALLY	I'd like some more.
MARK	No, it's okay.
SALLY	I want more.
MARK	Mom, she loved dinner. Really.
SALLY	Yes, Mrs. Gee. It was fantastic. I loved the presentation. It was so authentic.

LI FEN gives SALLY the thousand yard stare.

KIM	You too kind.
MARK	She's one in a million.
SALLY	Oh Mark.

SALLY grabs MARK's hand. LI FEN sees it. Crash of gong.

SALLY	We'll always be together, Agent Banana.
MARK	I'd sell my mother's heart to be with you, sweet Snow Princess.
LI FEN	Kim, take them to the Chamber of a Thousand Horrors.
KIM	I hear and obey, mistress of evil.
SALLY	Let me go!
MARK	Don't hurt her.
KIM	What else would I do in a torture chamber?

> *LI FEN clears the table and exits as KIM shoves MARK and SALLY to the back. They watch in terror as KIM transforms the kitchen table into a torture rack. They scream.*

SALLY   Noo...

> *Crash of gong.*

...kidding. This is an amazing acupuncture table, eh Mark?

MARK   It's okay.

KIM   Hmph.

SALLY   Well, Mr. Gee, I think it looks impressive.

KIM   Brand new. Real imitation leather. Looks good, but doesn't cost as much.

MARK   We should go, Sally.

KIM   Feel the table. Soft. Comfortable. Good, huh?

MARK   Dad, one table is just like another.

KIM   Aiya, what do you know? Sally, guess how much I pay for this.

SALLY   One thous–

KIM   Fifteen hundred dollars.

SALLY   That's a bargain. Good for you.

KIM   I knew someone would appreciate it.

SALLY   Mr. Gee, did you read the *Sun* last week? The university is planning to add acupuncture to its medicine programme.

KIM   Hmph, only a foolish man would give away his secrets. Acupuncture is a family art. My family passed down their secret techniques to me. It is a gift. How can any one treat it with disrespect?

MARK   Looks like you've got a rip in the "real" leather.

KIM   It's small. No one notice.

MARK   Guess that's why you got a deal.

KIM   Try the table, Sally.

SALLY   Oh, I don't know...

KIM   Go ahead. Maybe someone will learn something. I show you some acupressure, Sally. Okay?

SALLY   Alright.

SALLY gets on the table.

KIM   (*to MARK*) You watch...

Crash of gong. KIM pushes her down.

KIM   ...the infidel scream!

SALLY   Do your worst. I can take any torture. Flogging. Burning cigarettes. Even dripping water.

KIM   Dripping water? I like the sound of that.

MARK   Don't give him any more ideas.

Crash of gong as LI FEN enters with a plate of oranges.

LI FEN   Aiya Kim, stop that. She not one of your patients. Come eat dessert. I have oranges. (*to SALLY*) Orange help clear up your face.

SALLY   Thanks...

KIM   Eat later... (*to SALLY*) Let me look at your ear. Best way to know what is wrong with body is to look there.

LI FEN	(*to MARK*) How long you know Sally?
MARK	A year.
KIM	Mark, see these blood vessels. Stiff legs.
SALLY	They do feel kind of sore.
LI FEN	And you friends?
MARK	Yeah. Kinda.
KIM	Mark, pay attention. This bump means she has a pain in neck. Hold still. I get needles.
SALLY	Uh... isn't there something else you can do?
KIM	It's acupuncture.

> *KIM brings a box of needles to the table. It's a traditional box, ancient-looking, probably handed down many generations. He places it on the table beside SALLY and picks up a needle from it.*

LI FEN	Mark, what kind of friend is she?

> *Crash of gong.*

MARK	I'll never tell you, Yellow Claw.
SALLY	Uh, maybe give her a little hint.
KIM	I will prepare the needle of a Thousand Perforations, Yellow Claw.

> *KIM pulls on the needle so that it telescopes into one long mother of a needle.*

LI FEN	Tell me. What is this spirit you two share?
MARK	Something you'll never understand.
SALLY	The merest glance of him warms my icy tundra soul. One look fills my heart with joy. One peek

sends me soaring higher than the Royal Rocky Mountains.

LI FEN   Blind her.

KIM   Ah, the irony.

KIM is about to plunge a needle into SALLY's eye.

MARK   Stop it. She's done nothing to you.

LI FEN   You do not understand. She is the instrument of torture and you are the victim. You will watch as she crumbles from a mighty Canadian into a whimpering blind girl. This exquisite torture is for you.

SALLY   (*throughout LI FEN's speech*) Aiiieeee!!!

Crash of gong. SALLY's scream fades to a whimper.

KIM   Did I slip? Did it hurt?

SALLY   No. Not at all. I'm fine. No problem.

LI FEN   Where you meet your friend, Mark?

MARK   Did you know Sally works in the movies? She reads scripts.

LI FEN   What she do rest of time?

SALLY   It's a full-time job, Mrs. Gee.

LI FEN   Maybe she should learn to read faster.

MARK   Mom.

LI FEN   Why you never tell us about your friend?

MARK   (*Pause.*) Dad, let her off the table.

KIM   You like more acupuncture, yes?

SALLY   (*to LI FEN*) Actually, I think I've had enough for
               one night.

MARK   Leave her alone, Dad.

KIM   Time to learn.

MARK   I'm not interested in acupuncture.

KIM   No, you just play.

LI FEN   Not now, Kim.

KIM   Lazy. No good. Never do anything.

MARK   No, I just don't do what you expect me to do.

KIM   Same thing.

MARK   You can't force me to work in the clinic. (*beat*) You
               know I'm right.

               KIM exits, leaving his box on the table.

               Hey, we're not done talking. God, I hate it when
               he does that.

LI FEN   Your father look out for you.

MARK   Yeah, right.

SALLY   We should go.

MARK   Yeah.

LI FEN   I not done talking to your friend.

SALLY   I have an early start tomorrow.

LI FEN   She just do reading. What matter when she start?

SALLY   Mark, tell your mother, it's been interesting.

MARK   We have to go, Mom.

MARK   We have to go, Mom.
LI FEN   You stay.

SALLY   It was nice to meet you, Mrs. Gee.

            SALLY holds out her hand to shake LI FEN's hand.

LI FEN   Yes, it nice to–

            Crash of gong. LI FEN grabs SALLY's throat.

            Kill you! Infidel!

SALLY   Mmmfff. Agent Banana! Help!

LI FEN   Die! White devil!

SALLY   Agent Banana, what are you waiting for.

LI FEN   He will never turn against his own.

SALLY   He's not one of you any more.

LI FEN   You think, infidel?

MARK   Hiya!

            *MARK gives LI FEN a judo chop. LI FEN crumples
            to the floor.*

SALLY   Good work, Agent Banana.

            SALLY wraps her hands around LI FEN's neck.

            Now it ends.

MARK   Hiya!

            MARK hits SALLY with a judo chop. She crumples.

            Crash of gong.

            KIM walks to the acupuncture table, and opens the

are cast on the back wall. It is as if the generations of his family are watching over him. He works slowly at first, then more aggressive. Finally, he slams the table in frustration. He recovers, puts his needle in the box, and takes it off.

MARK and SALLY enter. They wear their trenchcoats.

MARK   You want me to rub it? (*beat*) Are you cold? Let's get out of the park. I'll give you a massage at my place.

SALLY   No, I think you've done enough.

MARK   What did I do?

SALLY   It's more what you didn't do.

MARK   I don't know what you're talking about.

SALLY   You didn't tell your parents about us.

MARK   You're crazy.

SALLY   No, I'm your friend.

MARK   That's just my mom's way of coping with it.

SALLY   The truth Mark. Did you tell your parents we were seeing each other?

MARK   No.

SALLY   I knew it.

MARK   It's complicated.

SALLY   No, it isn't. You just open your mouth and tell the truth. I thought you were serious about us.

MARK   I am.

SALLY   Got a funny way of showing it.

MARK	I love you, Sally.
SALLY	Yeah, right. When it's convenient for you.
MARK	What do I have to do to show that I care about you?
SALLY	You had your chance.

Crash of gong.

MARK	Snow Princess. You have to believe me. I wish to defeat the Yellow Claw.
SALLY	Then why did you strike me when I had a chance to finish her?
MARK	I thought you were her. I need glasses. That's why I'm so squinty.
SALLY	Wait a minute. I thought squinting was a genetic flaw of your people. Like bad driving.
MARK	No, that's the Koreans. Damn them.
SALLY	You're lying, Agent Banana. Don't give me that inscrutable look. You're protecting the Yellow Claw.
MARK	I'm on the level, Snow Princess. There is only one way to be rid of the Yellow Claw forever.
SALLY	How?

Crash of gong.

MARK	Do you want to move in with me?
SALLY	Excuse me?
MARK	I think we should live together.
SALLY	You're insane.

MARK It's a good idea.

SALLY Mark, you couldn't even tell your parents about us. You expect me to believe you're ready for this kind of commitment?

MARK Just because I have a problem with my folks, doesn't mean I have a problem with you. Let's move in together.

SALLY Don't you need your parents' approval?

MARK I don't care what they think.

SALLY You sure you mean that?

MARK Yeah.

SALLY Then why are you so worried about what they think about me?

MARK I just wanted to – I wanted them to like you. You know what? It's not important. It's just the two of us now. I'd rather be with you and if it means my parents are pissed off, let them be pissed off. Sally, I want to spend my life with you. All of it. Not just the weekends. But the weekdays too. The nights. The mornings. The times you wake up with bad hair and morning breath. I want it all. (*beat*) I'm serious. You're the only one who matters to me now.

SALLY You know what this would mean, don't you?

MARK I'm not gonna push you, Sally.

SALLY This would be a big step. A real commitment, you know.

MARK I'm ready for it.

SALLY You really are crazy.

> *SALLY walks away. MARK waits a beat, then follows.*

Crash of gong. KIM carries LI FEN in his burly arms. He lays her on the table.

KIM   Sweet task master. Please wake up. If you are dead, what will I do? Who will carry out our plans for world domination?

LI FEN   Oh – Kim Gee.

KIM   Yellow Claw!

LI FEN sits up.

LI FEN   What happened?

KIM   It appears that the infidels have escaped.

LI FEN   How could you let them?

KIM   They were with you last.

LI FEN slaps KIM.

KIM   I mean, I have no excuse for my incompetence.

LI FEN   Where are they now?

KIM   Gone in the labyrinth of a thousand twists...

LI FEN   Find them.

KIM   And kill them!

LI FEN slaps KIM again.

And bring them back?

LI FEN   The boy still has many uses, even if the girl has corrupted him.

KIM   He is gone to us.

LI FEN   But not his seed. He can produce many children, ones that we can raise properly. To be demur, inscrutable and totally subservient to me.

KIM   You are always thinking of the future, my evil
               empress.

               *Crash of gong. KIM wipes the table with a cloth.
               Across from him, LI FEN picks up the handset of a
               phone. She dials.*

DRUMMER   (*voice over*) This number is not in service. Please
               check your directory or call zero for assistance.
               Thank you from Telus.

               Li Fen hangs up.

KIM   Don't worry, he will come back.

LI FEN   Maybe something happen to him.

KIM   His landlady said he moved out.

LI FEN   Why she not know where Mark go?

KIM   He didn't tell her.

LI FEN   I don't think this happen if he had money.

KIM   He has to earn it, Li Fen.

LI FEN   Does it have to be in clinic?

KIM   This is where he belongs.

LI FEN   Maybe it not for him.

KIM   He has no choice.

LI FEN   Why not?

KIM   He is my son.

LI FEN   Maybe we call the police.

KIM   No, it will look bad. What will people think?

LI FEN   We should go look for him.

KIM	No.
LI FEN	You come. I need you show me where to go.
KIM	You should get to know city better, Li Fen. You can't stay in Chinatown all time. I will not be here forever.
LI FEN	You not help me look for him?
KIM	No. We lose face if people know our son has run away.
LI FEN	Mark might be hurt.
KIM	He will be back.
LI FEN	I think we should go look.
KIM	No, wife!

Silence.

	Li Fen, all we can do is wait for him. You know how to do that. You have lots of practice.
LI FEN	I don't know what you talking about.
KIM	I saw you Li Fen. I remember one time I got up early to get ready in clinic. Mark was out very late. And I saw you sitting in living room, waiting for him. You must have been up all night. We do the same thing now. Wait.
LI FEN	He might need us.
KIM	He will call us when he is ready to.
LI FEN	How can you be sure?
KIM	When he runs out of money, he will call.
LI FEN	I go look for him by myself. I don't need you.

KIM   Go. I won't stop you.

> *LI FEN looks at KIM. Then she summons the courage. She heads off, comes back with a jacket and heads for the front door.*
>
> *She stops at the door. She looks out. The faint sound of street noises. LI FEN can't go outside. She looks at KIM, who exits.*
>
> *The phone rings. LI FEN rushes to pick up the phone.*

LI FEN   Wei? Hello? Who is this? Hello?

> *Lights crossfade to MARK on the other side of the stage with a cordless phone. He hangs up. A beat. Then he dials the phone. SALLY enters.*

SALLY   Calling your mistress?

MARK   Yeah, your grandma says hi.

SALLY   At least you're keeping it in the family.

MARK   It's the least I can do for you.

SALLY   So who were you calling?

MARK   I was just following up my resumes.

SALLY   Give it time. Someone will call.

MARK   I hope.

SALLY   Maybe the feng shui in the apartment is off. That's why you're not getting calls. Let's move the chairs and adjust your luck.

MARK   You're nutty.

SALLY   Come on, Mark.

> *MARK moves the chairs as per SALLY's instructions.*

Start with that one. Yeah over there. Good. Maybe another one. Lift from the knees. Yeah.

MARK   I feel so lucky right now.

SALLY   One more. Good. Something's missing over here. Move that chair. Great.

MARK   You know, rubbing a rabbit's foot is a lot easier on the back.

SALLY   Yeah, but how else am I supposed to look at your great ass?

> *MARK gives her a look, then plops on the floor.*

MARK   You owe me a backrub for all that.

SALLY   Your parents into feng shui?

MARK   Yeah, their luck changed when I moved out.

SALLY   I should ask them for some advice.

MARK   They'll never tell you.

SALLY   Bet I could get it out of them.

MARK   You'd lose.

SALLY   What say we have an apartment warming party?

MARK   I don't think I can afford it.

SALLY   Pot luck. Doesn't cost us a cent. And we rake in some cool house warming gifts.

MARK   Now you're talking.

SALLY   Great. I figure we invite people with lots of money and good taste. That way we get a bigger haul.

MARK	Invite your boss. She's loaded.
SALLY	Have you seen how she's decorated her office?
MARK	Then your mom. Alimony must have been good to her.
SALLY	Yeah, but we invite my family, we'd have to balance it off.
MARK	Why?
SALLY	Why should I be the only one who suffers?
MARK	Forget the parents.
SALLY	Chicken. Why won't you invite your parents? They're probably dying to see our place.
MARK	My mom and dad aren't social people.
SALLY	They're probably just shy. It's that whole polite Chinese manners thing. They'll loosen up once they get here. I'll even order some Chinese take-out to make them feel at home.
MARK	It's not worth the effort.
SALLY	You know they haven't even called.
MARK	It doesn't matter, Sally.
SALLY	They're not having trouble with the idea of us, are they?
MARK	My family is not going to screw us up.
SALLY	I'd just like to know if there's something I can do to change their minds.
MARK	No. Nothing. Just drop it.
SALLY	Maybe I should have them over for Oolong tea. Let them see how we're doing.

MARK	That's the worst thing you could do.
SALLY	Why?
MARK	It just is.
SALLY	I'll bet if we just talked to them.
MARK	Just leave them be, okay?!!
SALLY	Okay. Okay.

MARK exits. SALLY watches him, puzzled.

A soft ring of the gong as SALLY transforms into Snow Princess. KIM enters.

KIM	The canary flies the coop at midnight.
SALLY	The panda devours her cubs.
KIM	The cocoon suffocates the butterfly.
SALLY	The young tree has deep roots.
KIM	Snow Princess. I'm the real double agent.
SALLY	I knew it. But then what is Agent Banana doing?
KIM	He's playing you. You're a cello to his Yo Yo Ma.
SALLY	I knew I never should have trusted him. All those Chinese are shifty eyed.
KIM	Once a minion of the Yellow Claw, always a minion... eh?
SALLY	Yeah, their kind never changes.
KIM	Ahhhh... sooooo. (*Chinese accent*) We never change.

KIM advances menacingly.

SALLY   What do you mean by– Wait a minute! You're no double agent.

KIM   I've always served the Yellow Claw.

SALLY   Is Agent Banana on your side or mine?

KIM   Yes and no.

SALLY   You're trying to confuse me.

KIM   No, I'm trying to kill you.

> *KIM chases SALLY. She stops him with a raised hand.*

SALLY   Maybe we can strike a deal. You don't have to sweat under the oppressive thumb of the Yellow Claw. You can come to Canada. Own your own restaurant. Or even a laundromat. Use your ancient Chinese secrets for good. The sky's the limit.

KIM   Could I become Prime Minister?

SALLY   No, but your children could become engineers or accountants.

KIM   Could they become Prime Minister?

SALLY   How about Governor General?

KIM   Aiee!

> *KIM charges after SALLY. He catches her.*

Okay, okay, okay. Tell me what you desire and I'll give it to you.

KIM   I desire to hear you scream!

> *KIM bear hugs SALLY.*

Crash of gong. KIM examines SALLY's back.

You come at right time. Stress getting worse. Acupuncture will relieve it.

SALLY   I was hoping for acupressure. I'm still a little needle shy.

KIM   I can do that.

SALLY   So how's business?

KIM   Always busy.

SALLY   Yes, I can imagine. Acupuncture is becoming more and more accepted as real medicine.

KIM   When has it not been?

SALLY   I mean in western society.

KIM   Nice to know west is catching up. You want tea? I get my wife to make some.

SALLY   No, that's fine. Just the acupressure. It's my neck that's killing me.

KIM   I take care of it. Lie down.

SALLY climbs on the table. KIM gives her a massage.

SALLY   Ah, that's great. Sometimes, I wish Mark would follow in your footsteps.

KIM   Make two of us.

SALLY   Maybe he'll come around. Never know what he's thinking.

KIM   He very quiet. Never talk much.

SALLY   Actually, I can't get him to shut up.

KIM   You talking about my son? I never would believe.

SALLY   He's always full of surprises. I never know what
             to expect. I mean, he's Chinese, but he's not. First
             date, we went to a Chinese restaurant. I had to
             order, because he didn't know how to read the
             menu.

KIM   He never liked to learn. He try to be different all
             time.

SALLY   I kinda like that about him. He's never boring.
             Frustrating sometimes, but never boring. I like
             never knowing what to expect.

KIM   You get tired of it soon.

SALLY   So have you talked to him?

KIM   You see Mark?

SALLY   You haven't?

KIM   We not see him for two weeks now.

SALLY   I'm sure he's been busy. Maybe if you called him.

KIM   We don't know where he is.

SALLY   What do you mean?

KIM   He moved out of his apartment. He did not say
             where he go.

SALLY   You're serious?

KIM   I think he run away from home.

SALLY   That's so irresponsible. How could he do this?

KIM   My son is hard to understand sometimes. He
             never tell us what he do. He get in trouble, he
             deal with it himself. He try so hard to show he
             not need us. He very stubborn.

SALLY	And stupid.
KIM	His mother is very worried.

SALLY gets off the table.

SALLY	He'll turn up sooner or later.
KIM	She just want to know he is okay.
SALLY	I'm sure he is.
KIM	If you see him, tell him to call us.

Crash of gong.

SALLY	I won't rest until the Yellow Claw is annihilated.
KIM	You will never succeed alone.
SALLY	As long as Mark Gee is at my side, I cannot fail.
KIM	Agent Banana will see the error of his ways.
SALLY	Mark is a true Canadian now.
KIM	He is an immigrant.
SALLY	What other kind of Canadian is there? We will treat him with the dignity that we treat all our immigrants. Even the Native Indians.
KIM	You would not if you knew the truth about him.
SALLY	I know about his past.
KIM	Not all of it. Did you know he is the Yellow Claw's heir. He is our son.
SALLY	That's impossible.
KIM	Do you think we look alike for no reason?

SALLY   You lie.

KIM   Choose not to believe me. Choose to ignore our straight black hair...

SALLY   No.

KIM   Our almond shaped eyes with brown centres...

SALLY   It can't be...

KIM   Our jaundiced skin...

SALLY   Can it?

KIM   He was sent to subtly infiltrate your ranks like MSG in Chinese food. Gain your trust. Then when the moment is right, he will strike you down like uncooked pork.

SALLY   No!

> *KIM laughs as SALLY runs away. He chases after her, laughing all the way.*

> *Crash of gong. MARK enters, chuckling at a script he is reading. He looks up and sees SALLY at the door. She's pissed off.*

MARK   Hey this script is pretty funny. Wrath of the Yellow Claw. You gonna recommend it?

> *SALLY grabs the script from him.*

SALLY   That's confidential material.

MARK   It was just sitting on the dresser.

SALLY   Of all people, you should understand what it means to keep secrets.

MARK   What's wrong?

SALLY	My scripts are off limits.
MARK	I'm sorry.
SALLY	I don't like people going behind my back.
MARK	I said I'm sorry. Now that I know, I won't touch your scripts. (*Pause.*) You know this one's pretty good. I laughed more than a couple of times.
SALLY	What do you know about screenplays?
MARK	I know what I like.
SALLY	You find Asian stereotypes and racist jokes funny?
MARK	It's a send up.
SALLY	It marginalises the Chinese.
MARK	What?
SALLY	It makes everyone think Asians are villains and buffoons. The Chinese are more than that. They're immigrants who've suffered and sacrificed for a better life here. And I don't support any script that degrades their collective experiences.
MARK	When did you become an expert on the Chinese?
SALLY	We've outgrown these kinds of stereotypes.
MARK	Seen a Jackie Chan flick lately?
SALLY	I'm just saying that writers should never be allowed to make up these offensive caricatures.
MARK	He didn't make them up. I've seen these stereotypes since I was a kid.
SALLY	This guy shouldn't be writing about Chinese people. He's not Asian and that's misappropriation of voice.

MARK	That's big of you to speak for my people.
SALLY	This guy shouldn't be writing about this.
MARK	So what if the writer was Chinese?
SALLY	They should leave these stereotypes behind. It's just going to give racists permission to use these awful jokes themselves.
MARK	I didn't know racists needed permission to be assholes.
SALLY	I mean let's not to invite discrimination back into our lives.
MARK	Who said it left?
SALLY	It's better not to have reminders of it.
MARK	No, it's better to have everything out in the open.
SALLY	You're one to talk.
	Crash of gong.
MARK	How dare you accuse me of betrayal, Snow Princess. I risked my life to join your side.
SALLY	No, you've peeled away your yellow skin and revealed a rotten banana inside.
MARK	I don't know what you're talking about.
SALLY	Don't play dumb, Agent Banana. You are the Yellow Claw's heir.
MARK	Where did you get such a crazy idea?
SALLY	Kim Gee. Your father!
MARK	(*Pause.*) Snow Princess... that was in the past.
SALLY	They are your family.

MARK	I've turned my back on their ways. I've cut my pigtail. I've let my math skills slip. I've torn down all my Bruce Lee posters.
SALLY	You can't change who you are.
MARK	Yes I can. How can I show you?

Crash of gong.

SALLY	You can start with the truth, Mark. Why didn't you tell your parents about us?
MARK	I was working up to it.
SALLY	So you ran away from home and you didn't even have the guts to tell me.
MARK	I'm sorry, Sally.
SALLY	Why didn't you tell me?
MARK	I thought I'd tell them before you found out.
SALLY	And that's supposed to make me feel better?
MARK	I was just trying to find a way to break it to them.
SALLY	It's simple. You just tell them.
MARK	My parents are different.
SALLY	That's crap and you know it. I sucked it up and told my dad and mother.
MARK	And they took it so well.
SALLY	The world didn't end, did it? Mark, I care about you, but this thing with your parents is getting to be too much. I don't know why you're so scared of them.
MARK	My mom hasn't heard of couples living together. She comes from an arranged marriage.

SALLY   So?

MARK   She expects a wedding to come before living together.

SALLY   Times change.

MARK   My mother doesn't.

SALLY   You haven't given her a chance to.

MARK   She's really traditional.

SALLY   Yeah, but she's in Canada now. She must have had some inkling that you'd end up with someone like me. I mean why come here if you don't want to be Canadian.

MARK   Just trust me. She'd never understand us living together.

SALLY   Oh? You know this from experience? So how many girls have you lived with?

MARK   That's not the point.

SALLY   You're right. The point is that I trusted you enough to let you move in with me. And you broke that trust before you could unpack.

MARK   I'll make it up to you.

SALLY   Are you ashamed of me?

MARK   No. I just couldn't figure out how to tell my parents.

SALLY   Mark, everyone gets scared. But grown-ups learn to deal with their fears.

MARK   I'll tell them. I promise.

SALLY   I've got work to do.

MARK	I mean it. I'll tell them.
SALLY	Yeah, right.

SALLY exits.

MARK	Sally, I will tell them.

Crash of gong. KIM enters.

KIM	The infidel has lost trust in your words, betrayer. She has heard the truth.
MARK	Now I have no one.
KIM	We welcome you back. The Yellow Claw needs you to complete our plans of world domination.
MARK	You won't take me without a fight.
KIM	So be it.

MARK unleashes a few impressive kata moves, supplying his own sound effects.

DRUMMER	(*as KIM lip synchs*) I see you have studied with Shaolin Master Way Wong. Well, here are a few tricks he did not teach you. Crane standing on one leg ready to swoop. Aieeee!

KIM resumes speaking. MARK and KIM pose, but never make contact with each other.

MARK	I counter. Tiger with unsheathed claws.
KIM	Mongoose with buck teeth.
MARK	Owl with whiplash.
KIM	Snake with arthritis.
MARK	Dog about to pee. Ouch, cramp!

left to right:

*Patrick
Gallagher,
Caroline
Livingstone,
Jared
Matsunaga-
Turnbull.*

*photo by Ian
Jackson*

KIM	You fought well, betrayer. But none have bested me in hand to hand combat.

KIM shoves MARK to the table.

MARK	You must tell me. Who was your kung fu master?
KIM	David Carradine. Yellow Claw!

Crash of gong. LI FEN enters.

LI FEN	Why you call me, Kim... Aiya, Mark. You come home.
MARK	Hey, Mom.
LI FEN	Are you okay? You not in trouble?
MARK	I'm fine.
LI FEN	You sure?
MARK	Yes.
LI FEN	Aiya! So skinny. You need to eat. I make dinner.
MARK	I'm not hungry.
LI FEN	It good you home.

She strokes his head.

MARK	Quit it, Mom.
KIM	Where you go? Your mother was worried.
MARK	Nice to see it didn't affect you any.
LI FEN	Why you not tell us where you move?
MARK	I had some things to work out.
KIM	What could be so important that you could not tell us?

MARK   It's complicated.

                Crash of gong.

LI FEN   Do you really believe the white devil's promises
                to allow you to join the westerners?

MARK   Yes, Yellow Claw.

KIM   You will always be an outcast there.

MARK   I am an outcast here too.

LI FEN   They see you as a lackey.

KIM   That is the worse fate in the world.

                LI FEN glares at KIM.

                For some people. You will never fit in there,
                betrayer.

MARK   I'm willing to do anything to be in Canada. Even
                learn their clumsy non-musical language.

LI FEN   Tell me, did the white devil say your family could
                go to the gold mountain?

MARK   You know I would never bring you.

KIM   You are ashamed of us.

MARK   You're evil.

LI FEN   He has turned from us.

KIM   A small matter that can be rectified.

                KIM pulls out a long needle.

                Shall I, Yellow Craw?

LI FEN   I have something better planned. But remain
                close by. I may need you.

KIM   I will stand here and contemplate the number of angels that can dance on the head of this pin.

LI FEN   Twelve.

KIM   You are infinitely wise, Yellow Craw.

MARK   Claw not craw.

LI FEN   Silence. Now tell me what did you and the white devil have in store for me?

  Gong.

MARK   Mom, Dad, there's something I haven't been telling you. It's about Sally and me.

  Gong!

KIM   Again with the girl.

LI FEN   His spirit cannot be broken as long as the girl is alive.

  GONG.

MARK   We're in love.

LI FEN   Aiya, too young.

MARK   There's more.

  GONG!

LI FEN   What is this love?

KIM   A western concept.

LI FEN   Impractical.

  GONG!!!!

MARK   Stop that!

DRUMMER   Sorry.

MARK   (*to LI FEN*) I didn't tell you where I was living because... Mom, Dad, there's no easy way to say this.

KIM   Then just say it.

MARK   Sally and I are living together.

> *Ting.*

LI FEN   You have committed the ultimate betrayal.

KIM   Now you're really going to get it. Hee, hee, hee.

LI FEN   Kill him.

KIM   Right away– What? Don't we need him for the master plan?

LI FEN   Not any more.

> *Gong.*

MARK   Mom, Dad... we'd like you to come over to our place sometime. Here's the address...

> *He pulls out a piece of paper.*

LI FEN   What I do wrong? You not like this before.

MARK   What are you talking about? I haven't changed.

LI FEN   You have no respect for us. You cannot live with her.

MARK   I'm old enough to decide what's best for me.

KIM   Even if it mean you hurt your mother?

LI FEN   Move home, Mark.

MARK   No, Mom. I'm gonna live with Sally.

LI FEN	What kind of son are you?
MARK	One that has his own mind.
KIM	Selfish boy.
MARK	Can't you see this is important?
LI FEN	Go play with your cars and white girls. I don't care.
MARK	What are you saying, Mom?
LI FEN	You not welcome in my house any more. I have no son.

Crash of gong.

KIM	She cared about you. Like a mother panda watches her cubs.
MARK	Yellow Claw, you can't watch me all the time.
LI FEN	Apparently not.

LI FEN pulls out a chopstick from her hair.

KIM	Aiya, not the Chopstick of a Thousand Acids.

KIM scurries away as LI FEN advances on MARK.

LI FEN	Can you truly fight me, my son?
MARK	I'll do what it takes.
LI FEN	Even kill your own mother?
MARK	We were never close.

LI FEN lunges at MARK. They struggle. LI FEN staggers back with the chopstick in her stomach. She chokes and gags as she backpedals.

LI FEN	But you are yin to my yang. Ping to my pong. We are inseparable.
MARK	I have an adopted mother now, and her name is Canada.

Upon hearing these patriotic words, LI FEN falls on the table and dies, leaving us to wonder what really killed her. The chopstick or her son's rejection.

KIM	How could you kill the Yellow Claw?
MARK	I did what had to be done.

MARK goes offstage. KIM tries to revive LI FEN.

KIM	Mistress of malice? Empress of evil? Yellow Claw?

MARK returns with a funeral cloth.

MARK	Leave her. She is gone to us.

A rhythmic beat of drums. MARK offers the cloth to KIM. Together, they drape LI FEN's corpse with the cloth. The chopstick juts up, making the cloth tent up.

KIM	What will I do now? Who will complete our plans for world domination?
MARK	Is that all you care about?
KIM	What else is there? Aiya!!!

KIM rips the cloth from the table. LI FEN is gone. Only her dress remains behind.

MARK	What!?
KIM	Mistress?

KIM pulls up LI FEN's dress.

KIM   Yellow Claw?

               Grains of rice pour out of the sleeve.

               AIIIIEEE!!!

               Crash of gong as lights come down.

ACT TWO

> *Lights up. MARK stands centre stage. SALLY and LI FEN grip each one of MARK's arms. A grinding sound echoes throughout.*

SALLY   Get away from him Yellow Claw!

LI FEN   He is mine, infidel.

MARK   I killed you!

LI FEN   I forgive you.

SALLY   Let go of him.

LI FEN   Never.

MARK   You're both hurting me.

> *KIM appears as a giant shadow on the rice screen.*

KIM   That pleasure will be mine. Ha, ha, ha, ha.

MARK   Get away from me. All of you.

SALLY   Canada beckons you, Agent Banana.

LI FEN   I open my heart to you, son.

KIM   Accept your place in the scheme of things, minion.

MARK   (*sings*) Oh Canada, our home and native land!

KIM   Nooooo!!!!

> *KIM's shadow washes out. The women pull hard. Pop! The arms come off MARK.*

MARK   AHHHH!

> *MARK stands between the women without his arms. He gapes in horror.*

> *SALLY runs her fingers through the veiny bits of the arm. LI FEN cradles her arm like a newborn.*

SALLY   Agent Banana.

LI FEN   My son.

SALLY   My lover.

> *The women look to each other. They advance on one another and beat each other with MARK's "unattached arms". MARK falls to the table in the scuffle.*

LI FEN   Stay away from my boy.

SALLY   You gave him up.

LI FEN   I want him back.

SALLY   He can never be yours.

LI FEN   If I can't have him, no one can.

SALLY   Desperate words from a powerless dragon lady.

LI FEN   I brought him into this world, I can take him out.

> *LI FEN holds "MARK's arm" high over her head with both hands.*

SALLY   Two can play that game.

> *SALLY imitates LI FEN. Simultaneously, they smash the unattached arms against their own knees, breaking the arms like dry twigs. There is a sickening crunch.*

> *MARK bolts upright screaming. His arms are intact.*

MARK   Ahhhh! What an awful nightmare.

> *KIM pops up from behind the table.*

KIM   Your nightmare is only beginning. You will pay for what you did to the Yellow Claw.

MARK   I'd do it again if it meant an end to her evil reign.

KIM   You won't have the chance to do anything ever again.

SALLY   (*off stage*) Meow!

MARK   Did you hear that?

KIM   What?

SALLY   (*off stage*) Meow. Meow.

MARK   It sounds like a cat.

KIM   Did it get out of the soup pot again?

     KIM heads to the exit and looks off stage.

     Here, kitty, kitty.

     Bonk! SALLY strikes KIM on the head. He falls. She drags him off, and then leaps on stage.

MARK   Snow Princess.

SALLY   Agent Banana.

     She kisses him on the cheek.

MARK   You saved me.

SALLY   I heard what you said. I'm sorry I ever doubted you.

MARK   It doesn't matter any more.

SALLY   Yes, you've shown your true colours, Agent Banana.

MARK   Yeah, and not a trace of yellow.

Crash of gong.

SALLY   Mark, there's still some left.

MARK   Well get it off, Sally.

SALLY   Hold on. Hold on.

Sally wipes Mark's face.

SALLY   There. Got it.

MARK   You ever think of using less lipstick?

SALLY   It's off. It's off.

MARK   Maybe I should wear my jeans.

SALLY   It's an interview. You look fine. When you get the job, you can wear whatever.

MARK   I'm gonna blow it.

SALLY   You're ready.

MARK   I don't have enough experience.

SALLY   You've got tons.

MARK   They're gonna ask for references, and then find out I got fired.

SALLY   Tell them what happened.

MARK   They're really gonna hire me after that. Sir, the reason why I was canned was because some jerk thought Chinks can't drive cars, so they probably can't fix them either.

SALLY   Then use my name as a reference. I'll be the head of Sally's Service Station and I'll give you a glowing recommendation.

MARK	Yeah, that'll be a big help.
SALLY	I'm doing what I can, Mark.
MARK	Just let me handle it. That way nothing can go wrong.
SALLY	(*Pause.*) Sure...
MARK	Where are my shoes?
SALLY	By the door.
MARK	Goddamn it. Can anything else fuck up today?

MARK heads off.

SALLY	It wasn't my fault.
MARK	What?
SALLY	You can't blame me for what happened.

MARK comes back with his shoes and puts them on.

MARK	I don't have time to talk about this.
SALLY	But you have plenty of time to make me feel like slug.
MARK	We'll talk about this when I get back, okay?
SALLY	You know, it was for the best. Now you can get on with your life.
MARK	What life? I'm two days away from welfare. I'm sponging off you. And I'm late for the only interview I've had in four weeks.
SALLY	Isn't this what you wanted?
MARK	Yeah, I really planned to be a loser.

SALLY   You're not a loser. You're going through what every twenty year-old is.

MARK   A screwed up life?

SALLY   No, a chance to make it on your own.

MARK   You're kidding, right?

SALLY   You think I didn't go through this? You think I just landed my job? I waited on tables for two years before I got my break. This isn't any different.

MARK   Yeah, it is. You can call for help.

SALLY   So can you.

MARK   How?

SALLY   Just ask me.

Pause.

MARK   Sorry. I'm stressed. You know, about the interview.

SALLY   I know what it's like, Mark.

MARK   Yeah...

SALLY   I know you'll do fine. I love you.

SALLY leans in to kiss MARK. He holds up a hand to stop her. She smiles and walks away.

MARK exits. KIM enters with the globe from the top of the play. He has one chopstick. He sits at the table.

KIM   The key is the entry point. Find the right one and we can reach the nerve centre. Strike where they are most vulnerable... the heart. Yellow Craw...

DRUMMER   Craw... craw... craw.

KIM gets up, looks around, but sees nothing. He sits down.

KIM   The plans for world domination must continue. Two worlds cannot coincide.

KIM pushes the chopstick into the globe. It pops! Now there is only a rice bowl in his hand. He starts to eat from the bowl with the one chopstick.

Crash of gong. KIM stops eating.

KIM   Aiya! Wife, I dropped my chopstick. Bring me another one.

LI FEN enters and slaps a chopstick on the table. She sits at the other end of the table.

KIM   Aiya! What is wrong with you?

LI FEN   S'ay h'am ga ch'an. [*Bastard.*]

KIM   I did nothing.

LI FEN   Hmph!

KIM   I did not make him move in with white girl.

LI FEN   This not happen if we stay in China.

KIM   Li Fen, you know we had to leave.

LI FEN   You had to go. I had no choice.

KIM   I couldn't leave you there by yourself.

LI FEN   There I had family. Here I have no one.

KIM   You can find friends.

LI FEN   Where? We never leave the house.

KIM	You can go by yourself.
LI FEN	(*Pause.*) It better in China.
KIM	No, now you have a better life.
LI FEN	Who say?
KIM	I do. You know I would have to close the business if we stayed in China.
LI FEN	You never asked me if I want to go.
KIM	It was for the best.
LI FEN	You always do what best for you, not anyone else.
KIM	You want Mark to grow up like us?
LI FEN	He be better off than he is now.
KIM	That has nothing to do with us moving here.
LI FEN	In China, I find good Chinese wife for him.
KIM	It is too late for that now.
LI FEN	You never should come here.
KIM	I cannot change anything now.
LI FEN	You mean you not want to.
KIM	What do you expect me to do?
LI FEN	Just what you always do. Nothing.
KIM	Wife. Don't talk to me like that.

The couple face each other. There is a definite distance between them. They exit.

SALLY enters. MARK enters behind her.

MARK	Say hello to the newest mechanic at Al's Auto.
SALLY	That's great, Mark. When do you start?
MARK	Next week.
SALLY	See? You had nothing to worry about.
MARK	Yeah, I can cover my share of the bills now. They're paying me two hundred more a month than my old place. And there's dental after a year. It's sweet.
SALLY	Welcome back to the work force. How about we go out for dinner to celebrate?
MARK	My treat.
SALLY	Oo, big spender.
MARK	Just call me deep pockets. In the mood for Chinese?
SALLY	Always. Wei, lo yut deep hi.
MARK	Excuse me?
SALLY	Wei? Lo yut deep hi? I thought I ordered crab.
MARK	No, you just came on to the waitress. Hai is crab. Hi is a woman's front bottom.
SALLY	What?
MARK	Crotch.
SALLY	Oh. Hi.... High.... Hai.
MARK	Better. Just remember. Down tone. Crab. Up tone. Down there.
SALLY	Hey, I know this great place downtown. The Kwong Tung. They make great lo mein noodles. Very authentic. Lots of Chinese atmosphere. The

waitresses refuse to speak English. So I can offend them with my Cantonese.

MARK   I was thinking of another place.

SALLY   Okay. Where?

MARK   Chez Gee.

SALLY   Your parents?

MARK   It'll be great. We'll walk right in and tell them I've got a job. I can't wait to see the look on my dad's face.

SALLY   Mark... they disowned you. Remember?

MARK   Yeah, but I wanna stick it to my old man.

SALLY   Just leave it be, Mark.

MARK   And pass up a chance to wipe the smug grin off his face? No way. It'll be great if you're there too.

SALLY   Why?

MARK   Because... they'll see we can take care of ourselves.

SALLY   I already know that. I don't need to prove it to someone else.

MARK   It's not about that, Sally.

SALLY   Then why the visit?

MARK   I don't need to go.

SALLY   That's not what I'm getting from you.

MARK   (*beat*) It ended weird. I wanted to be the one to finish it.

SALLY   Then go.

MARK   No, it's not important. I've got you. That's all that
                matters.

SALLY   You're sure?

MARK   Yes. I love you.

                Crash of gong. SALLY pushes MARK away.

SALLY   No time for sentimentality, Agent Banana.

MARK   But we've won! The Yellow Claw is dead.

SALLY   Yes, but there is one small detail that must be
                attended to.

MARK   I told you it doesn't get any bigger than that.

SALLY   No, not that. All I need is...

                *The DRUMMER throws a pair of coveralls to
                SALLY.*

                Thanks.

DRUMMER   Any time.

SALLY   (*to MARK*) Put these on.

MARK   Why?

                SALLY heads off stage.

SALLY   You'll see in a moment, Agent Banana.

MARK   What does this have to do with anything?

SALLY   It will make our victory complete.

                *SALLY returns with a bowl and a powder puff. She
                spits in the bowl.*

                Lean forward.

MARK leans into SALLY. She smears his face with white cream.

MARK I'm turning white? But how did you–

SALLY That's what happens when long grain rice meets Canadian saliva.

MARK Are you sure this is necessary?

SALLY You long to be embraced as a Canadian, don't you?

MARK Well, if you think this is the best way.

SALLY Stockwell Day thinks so. Assimilation is the only way. No longer will you be Mark Gee, minion of the Yellow Claw. Now, you'll be Sven Olafsen, Swedish shoemaker.

MARK Ja. Ja? Ja!

SALLY Good. Now, find a place to hide and let that set. I'll look for a car to take us out of this evil place.

MARK Can I drive?

SALLY Yeah right!

SALLY exits. KIM enters, unaware of MARK. MARK can't see KIM either. The two men set the table. Then they exit. MARK returns with a dolly and a worklight. KIM comes back with a folded cloth and some needles.

MARK goes under the table and hangs the worklight, while KIM works on an invisible patient on top of the table. MARK flicks on the worklight. They look as if they are talking to one other, but the table separates them from any eye contact.

KIM You have much stress. You are holding much back. We must relieve the pressure points and let energy flow.

MARK	Yeah, here's the problem. Oil pan's got a leak. I'm surprised the engine didn't seize with all the oil it lost.
KIM	You must learn to release anger, fear, sadness. It no good to keep inside you.
MARK	Well, the oil does no good sitting on the ground. It's got to grease the engine. Keeps things moving.
KIM & MARK	Good thing you came in when you did.

A heartbeat sound, beats faster and faster.

MARK	But I got to say, other than the pan, your car's in great shape. You take pretty good care of it.
KIM	Thank you. I proud of my work. If you care about something, you do it right.
MARK	Yeah, I know it's hard when you can't tell a gasket from a distributor cap. You don't want to futz with anything in case you make things worse.
KIM	But in time you get more, how you say, experience.
MARK	I guess I could show you a few things. But to show all the ins and outs, that'd take way too long.

The heartbeat stops. The two men talk to each other, through the table.

KIM	Sometimes, no matter how much you know, you have to trust your heart to know what is wrong and how to fix.
MARK	It'd just be easier if I just did it myself.

KIM   But sometimes your heart fails you. Then, you
             have to listen to the patient to find out what is
             wrong.

MARK   You'd have to be some great guy for me to spend
             my time trying to teach you. And you still might
             not get it.

KIM   That is a chance you must take. Usually it work
             out fine.

MARK &
KIM   Okay, you're all set.

             *MARK turns off the worklight and gets up. MARK
             and KIM make eye contact. For a second, both their
             shadows are on the back wall. Then the front light
             fades out, erasing the shadows. MARK exits, with
             the worklight and dolly. KIM wipes the table.*

             *A hushed ring of the gong. MARK enters, watches
             his dad work, then steps to the table.*

MARK   Hey, Dad.

KIM   Hmph. You run out of money?

MARK   No, I figured you might like to know that I got a
             job.

KIM   That pleases me to no end.

MARK   (*Pause.*) Nice needles. But the ones Lo Chang
             made were better. Whatever happened to him?

KIM   He bought restaurant.

MARK   Good for him.

KIM   Waste his talent. What is point to turn back on
             what you do best?

MARK   Maybe the restaurant is his dream.

KIM	He burns noodles. His pork is under-cooked. His dim sum is terrible.
MARK	You eat at his restaurant?
KIM	Yes.
MARK	Why?
KIM	We owe him for all the years he helped us. We never turn our back on people who need us.
MARK	Look, I just wanted to let you guys know that I'm going to be okay. (*Pause.*) Can you talk to mom?
KIM	She is upstairs.
MARK	I was hoping you might talk some sense into her first.
KIM	Your mother made it clear how she feels.
MARK	I know she'd see things my way if you talked to her.
KIM	What is point? You don't want to work here.
MARK	We're not talking about the business.... Oh God, is that why you're on mom's side.
KIM	You belong in the clinic.
MARK	You were using mom to get me back here?
KIM	She knows how important the family business is.
MARK	I can't believe you'd stoop this low.
KIM	The clinic is your duty.
MARK	No, it's yours.

Crash of gong.

KIM Betrayer, you don't understand anything.

MARK I know I'm sick of this place and it's time to flee.

KIM There will be no escape this time.

MARK I can beat you. I know your weakness.

KIM I have none. Now take your rightful place as the Yellow Claw's successor.

MARK I thought I'd go into music instead.

KIM What?

MARK Not a violinist or a pianist. I thought something more creative.

The DRUMMER strikes a sour chord on a banjo. KIM and MARK look at him.

KIM Perish the thought.

MARK How about the theatre? Actor. Director. Playwright?!

KIM Stop taunting me with non-traditional career choices.

Crash of gong.

MARK It's my decision.

KIM This is not about what you want. Mark, you are the last Gee. You must take over the family business.

MARK You can't expect me to do everything you tell me, just because I'm your son.

KIM We are family. We look after each other. My father look after me just like his father look after him. You must do the same thing.

MARK	Did your father expect you to move the business to Canada?
KIM	It was for the best. It would not last in China.
MARK	Doesn't look like it's going to last here either.
KIM	That is your decision.
MARK	I'm happy doing what I'm doing.
KIM	What do you know about happiness? You are too young to know better.
MARK	I know what I want.
KIM	Now. But some day, you will want a family. You will want to give your children the best things, because it makes them happy and that will make you happy. That is most important thing. To have family and be able to take care of them.
MARK	There's more to taking care of a family than making money.
KIM	I spend five years here by myself, save enough money to give you and your mother a better life. I do everything I can to take care of you. That is what family does.
MARK	Where's the room for my plans?
KIM	How can you turn your back on us?
MARK	I know what's important. Having the freedom to make something of my life. If I don't have that, I won't be worth anything.
KIM	If you do not have family you have nothing.
MARK	I was going to tell you the same thing.

Crash of gong.

KIM   Tell me what? What could you possibly say or do
             to hurt me any more?

MARK   My father never loved me.

             *KIM picks up a spear from the wall. He stabs at
             MARK, but can't push it into his son's chest.
             MARK grabs the spear and holds it to his heart.*

MARK   Go ahead. Finish it.

             KIM lowers the spear.

             *MARK turns and exits. KIM puts the spear on the
             table. He sees the bundled cloth and unfolds to
             reveal it has the Yellow Claw's dress. He picks it up.*

KIM   Cruel, cruel fate. You have taken away my
             mistress and my future. You are an eagle
             swooping upon my heart. Clutching it in your
             talons and squeezing it until it is a dry, lifeless
             organ. Do not stop. Peck out my eyes. I no longer
             need them. I have already gazed upon the future.
             Scratch away my skin for I have felt the supple
             caress of my mistress' hand as she struck me. Oh
             soft skin, slap me once more. Reveal your soft
             hand and point me to the path of conquest. Aiya!
             All our hopes... erased by one who was our own.

             KIM pins dress to the back wall.

             Oh, empty dress. You will hang here to remind
             me of what I can never have. Now my heart is as
             empty as your sleeve. All I have left is retribution.

             *Crash of gong. SALLY enters with her laptop. She
             sets it at the table and grabs a chair. She sits down
             at the centre of the table.*

SALLY   While the script delivers some moments of
             juvenile humour, the offering is light, banal and
             without substance. Because of its heavy reliance
             on racial stereotypes, the screenplay may be
             construed as racist and outmoded for today's

at the centre of the table.

SALLY   While the script delivers some moments of juvenile humour, the offering is light, banal and without substance. Because of its heavy reliance on racial stereotypes, the screenplay may be construed as racist and outmoded for today's politically sensitive viewers. Close the fist on the Yellow Claw. Do not consider this offensive piece for further development. Only a base audience would find this material funny. The ones we are targeting are too sophisticated. They will see this for what it really is. We are better than this script.

Lights down on SALLY. She exits.

Lights up on LI FEN. She is alone. She has a piece of paper in her hand. Figures take shape upstage. Only their forms are visible but not their faces.

LI FEN   Gno h'oi tai gno ji. [I'm going to see my son.]

VOICE 1   *(played by MARK)* Koe hai been do a? [Where is he?]

LI FEN holds up a piece of paper.

LI FEN   Nay gee do hai been do a? [Do you know where this is?]

VOICE 1   Ho yeun a. Nay dim yung hoi? [That's far. How will you get there?]

LI FEN   Gno dup bus. [I'll take the bus.]

VOICE 1   Nay si m'si gno che nay. [Do you want me to drive you?]

LI FEN   M'si. M'go. [No thanks.]

LI FEN looks at the paper. She is less comfortable, more nervous.

LI FEN   Excuse please. I lost. You know how to get here?

LI FEN	Where?
VOICE 2	Ask the bus driver.
	Now LI FEN is afraid, but tries to put on a brave front.
LI FEN	Excuse me, does this bussee go to here?
VOICE 3	*(played by KIM)* That's in Kitslano.
LI FEN	You go there?
VOICE 3	No.
LI FEN	Which bussee does?
VOICE 3	I don't know. Check the route map.
LI FEN	What that?
VOICE 3	Get off here and ask the next driver.
LI FEN	I just want to find this address. Please help.
VOICE 3	Can't help you. Now are you getting off or not?
LI FEN	Sorry. I not mean to bother you. Sorry.
	LI FEN is completely helpless and alone. She walks around, afraid. She ends up at one end of the table. SALLY enters.
LI FEN	Hello?
SALLY	Mrs. Gee?
LI FEN	Your door was open.
SALLY	Yes, I was just heading out.
LI FEN	Mark at home?
SALLY	He's at work. He's got a job, Mrs. Gee.

LI FEN	That good.
SALLY	Can I get you something? Chinese tea? Hot water on tea leaves, right?

Tense silence. LI FEN surveys the room.

LI FEN	Your apartment nice.
SALLY	Thank you.
LI FEN	How many bedrooms?
SALLY	One.
LI FEN	Aiya, too small.
SALLY	We like it.
LI FEN	It better if you have something bigger.
SALLY	We can't afford anything else right now.
LI FEN	I give you money. Get bigger place.
SALLY	Thanks, but we can manage on our own.
LI FEN	You know problem with my son? He never know what he really want. When he younger, he want to be teacher. He try to go to school all over Canada. Get away from here. But his marks never good enough. He not very smart.
SALLY	He's smart enough to be doing something that makes him happy.
LI FEN	I think he still not sure what he want.
SALLY	That's something for him to decide.
LI FEN	My son too young to know.
SALLY	That's your opinion.

LI FEN	(*Pause.*) I tell you something.
SALLY	What?
LI FEN	Stay with your own kind.
SALLY	Pardon me?
LI FEN	Mark deserve better.
SALLY	You don't even know me.
LI FEN	I know your kind. You sit at home when you should be working.
SALLY	I am working.
LI FEN	Reading not working.
SALLY	Are you for real?
LI FEN	You don't belong with Mark.
SALLY	I think he's got a different opinion.
LI FEN	Mark will see you for who you really are.
SALLY	His salvation?
LI FEN	His concubine.
SALLY	What?
LI FEN	When he sick of having sex with the *gwai miu,* he will look for real wife.
SALLY	I think you had better leave.
LI FEN	You only good for the bed. Nothing else.
SALLY	Please leave.
LI FEN	He will get tired of you. *Gwai miu.*

SALLY	Get out! Now!
	LI FEN exits.
	Crash of gong. SALLY stands alone on stage. A light strikes the Yellow Claw's dress hanging on the wall. SALLY turns to see it. There is the sound of evil laughter off stage. It sounds like LI FEN. SALLY looks around. The laughter stops.
	MARK enters. His face is no longer white. He has a Chinese finger puzzle hanging off an index finger.
MARK	Snow Princess, look at what I found.
SALLY	Don't fiddle with it. It's a trap.
MARK	It was hidden in the Yellow Claw's bed.
SALLY	No good can come from there.
MARK	I think it's a device to set us free.
SALLY	I said don't mess with it.
	MARK sticks his other finger in the puzzle. He's trapped!
MARK	Shit!
SALLY	It's a Chinese finger puzzle. The only way out is to let go.
MARK	I'm trying. I'm trying.
SALLY	Hey! What happened to your face?
MARK	It wore off.
SALLY	Just relax and let go.
	MARK finally gets free.
MARK	Want to try it?

SALLY	You're not serious about getting out of this lair.
MARK	Of course I am.

He pockets the finger puzzle.

SALLY	You're stalling.
MARK	Why would I do that? I long to leave just as bad as you.
SALLY	Then explain this!

She indicates the Yellow Claw's dress. MARK is shocked to see it.

Crash of gong.

MARK	I can't, Sally. My mom's never done this before.
SALLY	Well, she showed her true colours today.
MARK	I can't believe she'd do this.
SALLY	She just dismissed me because of the colour of my skin. If only you knew how that felt. It's reverse discrimination.
MARK	Why does it have to be some kind of special discrimination for you?
SALLY	You're right.
MARK	(*Pause.*) My mom's probably scared. I gotta talk to her and straighten her out.
SALLY	You can't talk sense into people like that.
MARK	You want her to keep hounding us?
SALLY	No.
MARK	Then what can we do? Move?

SALLY	Yes, and don't leave a forwarding address.
MARK	Look, the best thing to do is for me to talk to her.
SALLY	No, Mark. The best thing to do is turn your back on them. Just like they did to you.
MARK	They have to live with my decisions. They can't keep trashing my life.
SALLY	It's not worth it, Mark. Just walk away.
MARK	Sally, I'm not gonna let her get away with cutting you down. You deserve better. You're my girlfriend. (*Pause.*) We have to talk to her. Together.
SALLY	Forget it. I don't plan on going anywhere near that woman.
MARK	It's the only way to get her off our backs.
SALLY	Why do you care so much about what they think?
MARK	It's not that. I just don't want you to hold my mother's prejudice against me. Let's finish this.

Crash of gong.

SALLY	You've never finished anything in your entire life, Agent Banana. You're just a lazy, opium-smoking, laundry boy of the Yellow Claw. I'll wager you didn't even kill her.
MARK	I did. I swear.
SALLY	Prove it.
MARK	Kim Gee! Show yourself.

A deep drum roll. KIM enters with his spear.

KIM	Infidel! Betrayer!

MARK	It ends now. Tell her, Kim. Tell her how I killed your mistress.
KIM	The Yellow Claw is dead.
MARK	See? I told you.
KIM	Just as you soon will be.
MARK	You have no power against me.
KIM	No, but as you have taken away my mistress, I will take away the white devil.

> SALLY *pulls her eyes up, making them nice and slanty.*

SALLY	(*faux Chinese accent*) Oh no, so sorree. You have wong number. I no white devil. I just like you.
KIM	Why do you whiteys think a simple pull on your eyes can transform you into another race?
SALLY	I humble Chinese girl.
KIM	If I did not buy Jonathan Price as Vietnamese, I certainly will not fall for your flimsy disguise.
SALLY	I Chinese. My name Anna Chui.
KIM	Gesundheit!
MARK	No more cheap jokes.
KIM	Why not? It is the only thing her kind understands. Stereotypes.
SALLY	Hey, I'm Canadian. We're incapable of such low-brow thinking.
KIM	Mr. Moto. Charlie Chan. Here kitty, kitty. Time for soup pot.

> *SALLY doubles over with laughter. She stops when she sees no one else is laughing with her.*

SALLY   No fair. I wasn't ready.

KIM   You are ready for the grave now, infidel.

MARK   Stand back, Snow Princess.

KIM   Why protect her? You can easily buy another concubine.

SALLY   I'm not for sale.

MARK   We love each other.

KIM   Then her death will bring me the greatest of pleasures.

> *The two men square off in a Chinese stand off. KIM has his spear. MARK has his hands. Long pause.*

**KIM &
MARK**   Aieeee!!

> *KIM and MARK charge at each other. Cymbal crashes and percussion sticks beat. It sounds like a Peking Opera. The battle is fierce and fast, a Peking Opera style fight.*
>
> *MARK blocks KIM's spear, but gets knocked away. Before KIM can skewer the boy, SALLY intercepts him and goes toe to toe with the big man.*
>
> *Meanwhile, MARK grabs a spear off the wall. KIM is about to stab SALLY, when MARK arrives. The two men now fight, equally armed.*
>
> *MARK spins around, throwing kicks and jabbing his spear at KIM, who launches a series of counter-attacks.*
>
> *The music builds to a crescendo as the two clash in the middle of the stage. Suddenly the music stops.*

A light strikes the dress hanging on the wall. KIM and MARK backpedal. A slow click echoes their steps.

The cloth on the table rises up, up, up. A flash! The cloth forms a human figure standing on top of the table. A hand reaches out from under the cloth and pulls it off.

It is LI FEN! KIM and MARK drop their spears.

MARK   It's impossible.

KIM   It's glorious.

SALLY   It can't be.

MARK   She's alive.

KIM   *(to LI FEN)* Can it be you? Are my eyes deceiving me? How can I truly know it is you?

             LI FEN slaps KIM.

             My sweet villainous mistress.

MARK   But I saw you dissolve into rice.

LI FEN   I am not without my resources.

SALLY   You are a woman of many mysteries, Yellow Claw.

             Crash of gong.

LI FEN   That is why she does not understand our family.

MARK   Christ, I don't even understand you sometimes.

LI FEN   The *gwai miu* is not like us.

SALLY   Who says I want to be like you?

KIM   A good wife accepts her husband's ways.

LI FEN	She not his wife.
SALLY	And this isn't the stone age. God, why did we come here?
MARK	We're not getting married.
LI FEN	I don't care what you do with that *gwai miu*.
SALLY	Then why did you tell me to get out of Mark's life?
KIM	Li Fen, did you say that?
LI FEN	That *gwai miu* no good for Mark.
SALLY	I have a name and it's not white devil.
LI FEN	You come home, Mark. I look after you.
KIM	Listen to your mother. You have to be with your family.
MARK	This isn't China. I don't have to do anything you say.
LI FEN	Stay home. Out there no good.
SALLY	You can't have it both ways. You came to Canada, you have to take what it gives you. Just like Mark and me.

Crash of gong.

MARK	Yes, I reject my Yellow skin and embrace the white world.
SALLY	And we will welcome you with open arms.
KIM	She will take away your culture.
SALLY	No, we will sanitize his quaint customs and add them to our multicultural mosaic.

MARK	See how generous they are.
LI FEN	She is erasing your identity.
SALLY	Only the yellow bits.
KIM	The boy was raised to take over for the Yellow Claw.
MARK	I don't want anything to do with you.
KIM	Accept your destiny.
MARK	Accept my choices.

Crash of gong.

KIM	Selfish boy. You never understand what we do for you.
LI FEN	Kim–
KIM	Shut up, wife.
MARK	I never asked you for anything.
KIM	You didn't have to ask.
MARK	I don't need you. I've got Sally.
SALLY	Mark is old enough to look after himself.
LI FEN	Aiya, she no good for you.
KIM	She can't look after you.
SALLY	I don't have to.
KIM	You take him away from what he is meant to do.
MARK	Don't talk to her like that.
KIM	What do you see in her?
MARK	She's my way out of here.

    Silence.

    I didn't mean it that way.

SALLY	I'm a way out?
MARK	Sally, you're more than that.
KIM	No, you are just someone else he can use.
MARK	Stay out of this.
KIM	He will find another one when he is tired of you.
SALLY	You were using me?
MARK	It's not like that. Sally, you're the only one who's ever really mattered to me. I can't see my life without you.
SALLY	Or your parents.
MARK	I don't need to be here, Sally.
SALLY	We go now, we're never coming back. You understand.
MARK	Yes. Let's go.

    MARK and SALLY start to exit.

LI FEN	Stay, Mark. I need you.
KIM	When he run out of money again, he will be back.
MARK	I'm not coming back, Dad. You won't have to waste your money on me any more.
KIM	You will come back and you will learn to accept your duty.

    LI FEN grabs KIM and turns him around.

LI FEN	Just because he your son, you think he must do what you want. Just like you treat me.

KIM	Li Fen.
LI FEN	I your wife, but I have no say. You make me come to this strange place. You say you only want one child, I give him to you. I do everything for you.
KIM	Li Fen, we both give up everything to give Mark a better life.
LI FEN	You still have your clinic. All I have is Mark. Now you want me to give him up too? You never care about your family.
KIM	You don't know what you're talking about.
LI FEN	After everything your family do, you never go back to see them.
KIM	Li Fen, I wanted to go back as much as you did. But we had to save money so Mark have no worries when we are gone.
MARK	You were using me as an excuse to get away from your own family?
KIM	No.
MARK	Then why didn't you see your parents? Why didn't you bring them here?
LI FEN	Tell him, Kim. Tell him truth.
KIM	Not now, wife.
LI FEN	(*Pause.*) They did not think Canada was place to go. They want to stay in China.
MARK	(*to KIM*) But you still went? You mean you used them and then you abandoned them.
KIM	That is you, not me. It is your choice to abandon us.
MARK	No, it's my choice to live my own life.

KIM   Your life is my life!

LI FEN   Shut up! You talk, but you never listen. That is why you are losing your son.

    LI FEN turns to her son.

    Mark. Do what you want, but don't leave me alone. You are all I have. (*beat*) No matter what you do, I will care for you. Not because I have to. But because I want to.

    Crash of gong.

SALLY   Kill her.

    Crash of gong.

MARK   Didn't you hear her, Sally?

SALLY   Yeah, it's the same crap she's been saying since I met her. It's just part of her twisted game.

MARK   She stood up to my dad.

SALLY   She thinks I'm your concubine.

MARK   You don't understand what's going on.

SALLY   Them or us. What's it going to be?

MARK   (*Pause.*) I want you in my life. But I also want my family.

    Crash of gong.

SALLY   The only way to be embraced in the west is to turn your back on the east.

MARK   You want me to accept your world on your terms. You leave me no space for my own identity.

SALLY   Mark, you must shed your past if you want to come to Canada.

MARK	Then I choose not to go.
SALLY	You don't have to submit to her will.
MARK	I am exerting my own will.
LI FEN	You can leave, infidel. We will not stand in your way.
SALLY	This isn't supposed to be how it ends. The west is supposed to defeat the east. The girl is supposed to go off with the boy. The heroes have to win.
MARK	Aren't there any other endings?
SALLY	Why would you want anything else?
MARK	I'm sorry, but I do.
SALLY	I feel so sorry for you...

Crash of gong.

MARK	I'm sorry too, Sally.
SALLY	Okay, fine, whatever. Be her perfect Chinese son.
MARK	Sally, I love you.
SALLY	Yeah, I'm a great trophy.

SALLY exits.

KIM	You come home. It better for you.
MARK	I'm not coming home, Dad.
KIM	But you said–
MARK	I said I respect your sacrifices. It doesn't mean I'm going to take over where you left off.
KIM	You need us.

MARK   Just because I'm doing my own thing, doesn't mean I've forgotten what you've done for me. Just let me show my appreciation my own way.

KIM   After all this, you learn nothing.

MARK   Didn't you hear anything I said?

KIM   You have nothing good to say.

          KIM exits.

LI FEN   Mark, your father, he is set in his ways.

MARK   Yeah. I guess some people can't change.

LI FEN   Very hard to change. Only when it important.

MARK   (*Pause.*) Mom. When I get a new place, maybe you could come over and help me set up?

LI FEN   You need my help?

MARK   No. I want it.

LI FEN   You can take care of yourself.

          LI FEN exits.

          Crash of gong. Slowly, MARK's shadows form on the back wall. He does not notice them.

MARK   The panda lets go of her cubs. The butterfly climbs out of its cocoon.

          MARK notices his shadows on the back wall.

          The young tree has deep roots.

          Crash of gong. Lights down.

          The end.

Kicked out of engineering, fired from hot dog vending, Marty Chan was destined to become either a writer or a slacker. Marty enjoys exploiting his family, whether it be in his CBC radio commentaries or in his Gemini-nominated television pilot, "The Orange Seed Myth and Other Lies Mothers Tell." Marty hates pretentious bios and is scared of mustard.